Healing
Truths

Heal Your Pain And
Return to the Joy of Life

Healing Truths

Heal Your Pain And
Return to the Joy of Life

KEFAH BATES

Healing Truths
First published in Great Britain in 2022 by
LOTUS BOOKS
An imprint of PARTNERSHIP PUBLISHING

Written by Kefah Bates
Copyright © Kefah Bates 2022

A CIP catalogue record for this book is available from the British Library.
ISBN 978-1-915200013

Book cover design by: Partnership Publishing
Book Cover Image © Shutterstock 1829099090

Book typeset by:
PARTNERSHIP PUBLISHING
North Lincolnshire, United Kingdom

www.partnershippublishing.co.uk
Printed in England

Partnership Publishing is committed to a sustainable future for our business, our readers,
and our planet; an organisation dedicated to promoting responsible management of forest
resources. This book is made from paper certified by the Forestry Stewardship Council
(FSC) an organisation dedicated to promoting responsible management of forest resources.

To The
Beloved One.

Contents

Introduction

Understanding the nature of pain was not just my work but my calling. I carried intense pain inside of me, for others and the world for as long as I could remember.

Understanding why suffering existed was the only thing that felt real to me. I made it my life purpose to know why. I believed that suffering held us back from developing our higher potential and coming into deeper union with the divine source. While facilitating others to find meaning and move through pain, I came to profound clarity on the nature of suffering and uncovering the necessary conditions to transcend it. I wrote Healing Truths at a time when I was undergoing a deep realisation within myself.

What started as a profound wish to break every illusion of suffering developed into a spiritually transformative experience. Each truth derived from a peace that touched a realness penetrating deep into the heart.

These timeless teachings and personal reflections remind us that we emanate a light so unconditional and loving that all are free in its sight. 'Healing Truths' invites you to take from it all that touches your heart and to understand that your true essence awakens out of pain. What waits within is a real potential that delivers itself into loving union with the Holy and not against it.

"Courage is needed to explore the self
and master what is real."

Reflections

Throughout my life was the constant call to know freedom and God. I came to know both not from any religion or spiritual system but through mastering suffering in myself and others.

The following personal accounts reflect my own pain, struggle and movement towards self-empowerment, completion and oneness.

~.~

Inner Space

"The need to achieve can tie us in knots and deliver much frustration. The battle is not outside of us, but in the patience and courage to move past the need to be something."

Everyday life would seem so fast to me. It was a struggle, and often intense, so finding space away from everything was as essential as breathing. I couldn't be without it.

It would feel like such an effort to find enough space, to move out of everyday life and to have the energy to penetrate the shield. Being guarded and unsure was something I had experienced for as long as I can remember. The armour, the protection, and the high walls I built around myself, all served the purpose of keeping me safe.

Knowing how I genuinely felt about the life I was living only surfaced when I could move past the armour. It was when I was alone, whether in nature, in my car, or in sacred places that I found what I needed. I found peace and space for introspection, which would help me to pursue my deepest wish: to be free.

I don't think I could have ever imagined the extent to which my true self was buried. Only when I felt safe enough could my essence emerge. In time, my truth would reveal itself and I would come closer to the longing in my heart.

To take down the walls around my heart I had to turn inwards, to find out whether the fear in me was my identity. Out of fear and habit, it was difficult to leave the outer reality. My gaze was conditioned to move outwards and tend only to the many commitments I had. What would often seem a priority was just doing that which supported my personal or professional needs.

I cannot remember any memories when growing up that taught me that introspection was an integral part of health, inner harmony, and spiritual development. I was shown how to do so many things throughout my younger life, but not this.

I remember when I first began finding inner space. I would become so disheartened when I couldn't remain there for long. It was like growing a muscle that hadn't been used before. I knew I had to grow this muscle to develop deeper levels of awareness and connection with myself.

I realised that this muscle was my gaze. Initially, turning my gaze inwards was like an elastic band, I would pull it in and it would resist wanting to pull itself out. It was such a challenge to keep directing the gaze internally when all it wanted to do was remain in the external world. All our lives we develop and promote our gaze to look outwards, with emphasis on achieving and acquiring from outside of ourselves. No wonder it was a slow and gradual growth.

Going within, however, would become easier with practise, and over time I would navigate the distractions without effort. When going within, I would let my mind wander, without forcing anything, which was similar to daydreaming. After some time, I found that the distractions would slow down and the outside world would fade. I'd then start to become aware of how I was experiencing myself. This could be how my body felt, how I felt emotionally, or observing the thoughts in my mind. In this inner space, I could see the deeper me emerging, and in this seeing, I felt closer to who I was.

Seeing, sensing, and feeling the movement of me was a multi-dimensional experience. By observing my inner world, I would feel the sensation of me, listen to the sound of me, the breath of me, my urges and tensions, all of which were aspects of me.

I wanted to be aware of how I was responding to the impressions of life. I wanted the opportunity to see if what I was feeling was resonating truly. I would be shown what felt meaningful for me. In my everyday life I rarely felt I had enough time or space to reach this place. By creating the space, I could align myself and hear what really mattered to me.

In this space I reached a deeper knowing of myself that the surface self did not touch. Going within helped me to let go of the constraints of what I *thought* I should be.

I aimed to be as honest as I could and not to hold back, but to ask myself: what is happening within? What am I holding? Sooner or later, I would feel emotions and allow them to move through me. I would be shown what had touched me, what experience I had had that was making a lasting impression. I would recall what had generated emotion in my heart and what had moved me at that point. I became aware of impulses on the surface, noticing if they were making me feel good, sad, happy, or resistant. I would simply observe these movements within me.

With each inner inquiry there came insight that would help me discover my essence. Each time I explored my inner world I felt humility from being in touch with this deeper sensitivity. It felt like a great relief to experience such an intimate process within myself. What felt real to me came from this space.

~.~

I wasn't by myself in this struggle. Those who I treated found it difficult to meet themselves truly too. I realised that many people found it hard to be in touch with a deeper knowing within. This was reassuring to me, since the need to connect with an inner space in my life was not just a challenge for me, but for everyone.

It's such a powerful drive to give all our attention to what's created in our outer world. But when we only do this we lose touch with what is real within. The need to achieve can tie us in knots and deliver much frustration. The battle is not outside of us, but in the patience and courage to move past the need to be something.

Each time I reconnected with my heart, I felt the innocence of my inner child, curious, open, knowing the world through feeling, rather than thought. Many people fear the heart because a lot of the time what we feel is not logical or doesn't initially make sense to us.

Inner space allowed me to wander within the mystery of me, rather than knowing through the mind. I felt the freedom that comes from allowing my heart to be heard. I would breathe life into my soul and move past the surface noise and armour, turning my attention to what mattered.

To go within informed me of how I was sensing my world. This was my unique experience, which was true for me. When I met myself in this way, it was like coming home, I found peace and nourishment. I met my essence, where everything made sense.

Without expectation, finding space became a constant practise for me. It was like getting to know a stranger, each time I met myself in this way I would relax further, go deeper and embody who I was. This was my meditation, no force or control, just watching and learning.

Over time something extraordinary began to happen in how I related to the world around me. Because I came closer to what was real in me, I came closer to life and developed a deeper level of humility and care for myself and others. I could never have imagined that this exploration was laying the foundation for profound levels of spiritual growth.

I was no longer lost to the many interpretations of the source of me but came into direct union with it.

Helplessness

"To resist feeling vulnerable is the norm; we want to distract ourselves to escape it. It feels like we are exposing ourselves and we don't feel relaxed when we are vulnerable. Beyond our pain is a deeper message we need to hear."

When the emotional body was still an enigma for me, whenever I felt discomfort, pain, or discord, I would ask myself: why do I have to have such a difficult experience? Why do I have to feel this ache?

I wanted so much to get away from the heavy emotions in my heart. It would feel like a fight, something that was trying to break me, conspiring to bring me down. I felt like a victim because I didn't know how to get myself out of where I was, helpless and worried it would take too long, that it may take too much energy for me to try and hide the fact that I felt different from others. I saw pain as simply getting in the way of my life.

I would become anxious when I felt fear, pain, doubt, or worry, distracting myself with the question: why me? I would try to find the reason why misfortune was happening to me. I feared being a bad person and the expectation that others would not accept me this way.

In some way it feels effortless to adopt the role of the victim and feel helpless. We completely negate our fragile nature, that we are sensitive beings.

Instead of empowering myself through my sensitivity, I saw myself as weak and alone.

I repeated this cycle of learning each time pain came. Beginning with why me to then the disbelief that it was there, playing the role of the victim and then desperately trying to push away the pain to get on with life. This didn't change until I learned the true purpose of pain.

~.~

To resist feeling vulnerable is the norm; we want to distract ourselves to escape it. It feels like we are exposing ourselves and we don't feel relaxed when we are vulnerable. Beyond our pain is a deeper message we need to hear.

For us to feel exposed there needs to be something hidden. Therefore, when something is not hidden we can relax. Feeling vulnerable is not comfortable, but it does not mean we can't move through it or are helpless. Life is full of discomfort, which we can choose to move through and not suppress. I came to understand that to feel discomfort was a necessary step to experiencing what is authentic.

I realised by meeting pain that I was not a victim of life, only if I chose to run away from it. Accepting this was a big part of my healing journey. When the pain came, I would feel into the wound and come to understand myself. The pain would teach me about the blocks I was carrying, which had a deep meaning for me. I was learning how to accept the story of my life and to embrace who I was and not who I wanted to be.

Each time I surrendered to what pain was revealing to me, I moved into a deeper level of wholeness. I saw that life was not out to break me but to free my pain, pushing me beyond my limits.

My inner work would be for me a constant source of insight into the human condition. I often witnessed the response that many people have to feel pain, struggle, or discomfort. This could be to escape, to seek justice, to find someone to blame or to prove someone wrong. We can remain trapped in this victim mentality. But this remains a huge setback in the healing process.

Feeling like a victim protects us from feeling the pain inside of us. It buys us time and makes us blind to what is going on within. Pain remains in the shadows because we place it there. Something that we don't want to feel still exists even if we try to escape it. Playing the victim is the perfect decoy for not going within.

~.~

I wanted to change my response to feeling helpless. It began by accepting my initial response, allowing myself to vent. I knew it was what I needed to feel before I could tend to the healing process. I could either make it worse by judging myself or let it play itself out. Some part of me needed to cry about how imperfect I felt and once it had been heard I felt much freer.

It often felt that I had to experience many hurdles compared with others, who looked like they were living a perfect life. I realised that comparing myself with another only brought doubt into my life, which had no value in the healing process. I could choose to get lost in resentment and bitterness and consume myself with the pain of my hardship. The pain was a part of me, not by some accident or trickery, but for a higher good.

I began to explore a different approach. Instead of moving away from myself or suppressing this feeling, I decided not to abandon myself. This time I acknowledged that I was not going to ignore what was inside of me.

I had felt that pain was a hindrance in my life and that living with a constant feeling of vulnerability was debilitating. Wanting to ignore the natural way that the body heals had become so ingrained.

I understood that I was in fact ready for what was being revealed to me through the pain. I learned that it was no accident that pain was surfacing and that it was always going to happen. Life was not out to make me suffer. It was what I needed to find peace. If one bypasses meeting what lies beyond pain, then the opportunity for a deeper sense of wholeness is missed.

What is uncomfortable and painful is hard to see. Sometimes respite is essential on our healing journey, but pain lives inside of us for good reason, and it is not to disempower us. It may have felt that life was against me, but it was conspiring to help me realise that I was far greater than what I could see.

Meeting pain and discord within the healing process is more about taking the reins of the self and playing our part in it. Intense emotion exists because it has to, not because it is life's cruel infliction. I came to witness that suffering and helplessness were a choice.

Body and Soul

"Each time, I would approach myself as if I knew nothing, allowing the anxiety to lead me. The journey helped me face my deepest fears and I became the explorer of my own world."

Anxiety was a close companion throughout my healing journey. The symptoms of anxiety can be very different for everyone. For me, it was like having a constant heightened awareness of life, which was not comfortable to experience.

When I was younger I felt this anxiety more in the physical sense, in the agitation of the body. I was brought enormous relief when I found Yoga. It involved constant maintenance; if I missed one day, I would feel the anxiety come back even stronger.

I remember thinking that it didn't make sense to me that when doing yoga I felt relief in my body and soul. But then when I couldn't practise, anxiety was there again, like a never-ending well of tension.

Where did it come from, what was inside of me that made my constitution this way? Was it physical, or was it something deeper? At that time I felt that the more I did to bring health and peace into my life, the more that tension would reveal itself in other ways.

I came to learn that the healing journey was not how I wanted it to be. I believed that when I met anxiety with yoga that it would just go away, it would leave and never come back.

Yoga helped take the edge off the anxiety and agitation, but I had to find another way. The fact that it didn't go away would eventually lead me to want to understand why. I didn't just want to maintain my anxiety, I wanted to be fully cured of it.

~.~

I have always been in awe of the incredible resilience of human nature, especially when surviving painful and intense experiences. Healing wounds and understanding how to free the soul was a constant calling for me.

It is most common to want to rush through the healing process, to go as quickly as we can through anything that feels uncomfortable. We are used to tackling pain by numbing the senses and hoping that it will go away by itself.

In many cases, this is a huge relief, but it negates the fact that we are multidimensional, sentient beings, and to be whole we have to find a balance in our relationship with the whole of our being. Healing can't be about ticking a box, neither is there a magical pill for us to swallow to make everything go away. But there are deeper and higher reasons for pain existing in our hearts.

I knew curing anxiety was about understanding it. Anxiety comes in so many ways, through the physical it can be experienced as tension, stiffness, sickness, or agitation. Emotionally we can feel anger, fear, depression, or sadness. Mental disharmony could be paranoia, shock, worry, or shame.

These are only some of the distortions that rise when we become restricted by anxiety.

I wanted to run away from the discord and the fear, believing it would overwhelm me if I gave it too much attention. But it was when I stopped trying to make anxiety go away, instead allowing it to show me what it was doing, that my relationship changed. I came to realise that the discomfort from anxiety that I was so desperate to get away from had a purpose.

I began understanding anxiety by initially accepting it, so when I felt agitated, I would find space to stop and meet it.

Closing my eyes always helped me tune in to myself. I would notice if I could track when I started to feel the tension and the reason that triggered it. This was as simple as remembering what I had done in the last few hours, who I had met, and what exchanges had happened. Not knowing why I felt anxious made me feel disorientated, so it was necessary for me to adopt a compassionate approach centred on acceptance and introspection.

I would start to feel sentiments of support and love towards my anxiety and the symptoms I was experiencing. It was the same kind of affection as what I would give to a distressed child, except I was giving myself that care. I had to repeat this many times before something began to change.

The more I brought awareness to this sensitivity within, the more I actively opened and started to change the reality of the resistance I felt.

Then, later, one day, it became crystal clear: anxiety was preparing me to be still and to give myself attention. The discomfort it was creating in me was there because it was asking for my attention. When I gave it a deeper level of attention, then the surface anxiety went away, and I was shown the deeper reasons of why it needed to be there.

Anxiety and the symptoms of agitation, feeling vulnerable and sensitive, were not signs for me to shut down, but a kind of preparation. At a physiology level, my body became heightened as the anxiety grew. I felt highly sensitive and my body became so tense.

There came a point when I observed that the symptoms were so intense and uncomfortable that they forced me to stop, so I couldn't help but give it my full attention. Ignoring it was no longer an option. The stronger the tension or pain the more necessary it was for me to open.

Each time I consciously moved past the initial discomfort, some deeper emotion or understanding of how I was feeling would reveal itself to me. This was what anxiety was preparing me for, to meet that which lay beyond it. It was as if anxiety was transitory, and when I came to realise the source of my agitation, it subsided. It was the body's way of preparing me to be still, rebalance, and come to a deeper knowing of myself.

~.~

It can take time to steadily recover trust in ourselves. We become numb and ignore ourselves for good reason. If the path we have lived has overwhelmed our sensitivity, we will shut down our feelings as a necessity to keep us safe and to overcome the situation.

We are always growing and evolving, and the healing process teaches us this. It seems to be a major hurdle to accept our frailty, constantly showing the world a version of ourselves that we believe is more acceptable than what we are. We are not perfect, and if we fool ourselves that we are then this construct keeps us stuck. To recover trust in one's inner world is like opening up again to a dear friend we have not seen in a long time. It can't be rushed, but when care is shown, the bond we have with ourselves is sealed again.

Instead of anxiety feeling like a curse, I came to see it as the body's natural warning system, showing me that I was experiencing something that was not aligned with my sensitivity.

The healing process can feel very painful, especially if you feel imperfect. No one can tell you how long it will take to stop feeling pain. But with relentless perseverance and courage, I found it was possible to free my body and soul from the pain I carried.

By meeting discomfort, I consciously developed sensitivity. To unpack years of holding on to discord needs time, energy and space. When we feel overwhelmed and highly anxious, it is important to remember to stop, since anxiety is a warning sign that shows us that something is not right. Listening to this sensitivity and following where it's trying to lead is key to freeing ourselves.

~.~

Much of my work is helping people to understand that there are layers to healing, how to be present during the healing process, and how to slow down to meet one's true self. It may feel like we are not in control, but it is when we let go that we feel release. Emotion is energy, rather than a transparent figment of your imagination, and this is why it can feel overwhelming.

On my journey, I came to the stage where it didn't matter what form the discomfort took, whether anxiety, tension, unease, pain, pressure, I was going to commit to giving it attention, or giving myself attention to help ease it. Each time, I would approach myself as if I knew nothing, allowing the anxiety to lead me. The journey helped me face my deepest fears and I became the explorer of my own world.

Into the Darkness

"I came to understand that in healing, a great challenge is to let go of the attachment to what you are expecting, or what you feel you should become. It is crucial to understand the importance of letting go for spiritual growth and wellbeing. To let go is to realise that truth cannot lie in our expectations, but in what is."

It felt like at the core of me was a deep insecurity. It would show itself most whenever I felt lost and had to face the unknown.

If I was unsure of how to make the right decision, or follow one path over the other, confusion and a feeling of pressure to find the right path would come over me. This was often accompanied with panic, fear, and agitation.

It was often difficult to overcome these feelings. I couldn't simply make the right choice. Not knowing which choice to make, or what might come if it was the wrong choice, felt like stepping into the void, and it was the unknown that made me feel so uneasy.

I observed that when I felt lost, I felt empty. I had nothing to hold on to, I didn't know what came next, or what it would look like. At that moment I would feel that everything I knew about me might not be true, helpful, or valid.

The struggle was to let go and step into the darkness and not resist. Each time I tried to let go, and feel the emptiness, I would face a spectrum of emotions, which ranged from anything to grief, anger, sorrow, despair, or loneliness.

It felt like I didn't know who I was at that moment. It was painful because it was like facing an inner death each time. I desperately needed to hold on, but it became so much more difficult when I did. I would move between trying to reason it out and letting go. Neither option spared me from feeling discomfort.

Through my healing work, I was aware that when there was a significant issue that recurred in anyone, and was hard to shake off, this was so because it preceded a significant teaching. By applying this knowledge, I knew that facing the unknown was going to be important for my growth. I would have to face why it was so profoundly difficult to feel lost, to face the unknown, and to drift into the darkness.

~.~

What is the void we seek to escape? That which feels empty within is life's mystery, which promises something new that is not predetermined or pre-planned. To not know didn't feel exciting, it scared me and I wanted to remain in the known.

I felt lost because the void feels so unfamiliar. It feels scary going into this empty place inside because I believed nothing was there but pain and insecurity. It feels challenging to walk away from what feels familiar, to stand alone, and to choose to face the unknown.

I wanted to remain attached and distracted by the warmth and friendliness of the outer world, since this familiarity brings safety.

By entering the unknown, I wanted to control the experience, but in fact, to heal I was being asked to let go. Fear is relentless in trying to find a controlled outcome for the unfamiliar. But I found the stronger I held on, the more forceful I became in wanting control. Fear wanted me to not feel the pain in my heart, which was messy and unpredictable. I held on so much because the grief in my heart felt too much to bear.

The real challenge was to let go of knowing what was to come. To not know and yet still carry on is a profound practice of surrender, to come to the edge of everything you know.

In time, I realised that I had no choice but to feel these emotions. Yes, it was painful, and self-compassion was essential to help steer me through. Feeling intense emotion and its release came with a well of tears that never seemed to end. It's tiring, so finding space and supporting the whole self throughout is a constant learning process. Though it was difficult, with compassion it was bearable.

Through the pain, I realised that life was conspiring to help me and not to burden me.

I had lost trust in the deeper wisdom of my truer self and only regained it when I dared to go into the darkness and meet the pain. Clarity of inner knowing of oneself comes at the moment when the connection to the heart is open, and there is no expectation, just direct experience.

When I was able to move through the fear, I felt that there was a deeper movement within, no matter how subtle. I would go on to learn to trust the void and to realise that I was never lost. The pulse of life in the darkness, the creative life force in me was never still, I was never empty. To directly experience the fact that I was never alone was the game changer for me. By directly seeing what lay beyond pain, I came in union with a higher intelligence.

I began to trust this movement that was carrying me and to allow it to show me dimensions of myself that I had never known before. The void experience was an essential space that was helping me to let go. It helped me face my deepest fears of not knowing and feeling wrong for being there.

I realised that I was not lost or empty within. The belief that I could not overcome the fear of being in the darkness was what I believed in, and so blocked the way. What remained when I moved through the suppressed emotions was peace and an inner knowing that knew its way out.

When I was ready, when the pain subsided in every meeting I had with it, the grace of a higher force within showed itself to me. The journey can be long, and the wish to give in and to distract ourselves is strong. This was the test, only I could choose to know all of the parts of myself without knowing where it would take me.

This journey would reveal treasures along the way, which I could not experience in my outer world. Each level of pain I moved through delivered a personal truth that would bring about an unshakable self-belief. This would give me the sustenance to carry on and to unfold my true self.

I came to understand that in healing, a great challenge is to let go of the attachment to what you are expecting, or what you feel you should become. It is crucial to understand the importance of letting go for spiritual growth and wellbeing. To let go is to realise that truth cannot lie in our expectations, but in what is. Resisting going within to meet pain comes in many ways. For so long I sought answers outside myself. This was a habit, and so turning inwards felt like swimming against a strong tide, the effort needed is more than we realise. I see how people give themselves a hard time, turning against themselves for feeling as lost as they do.

To be lost is not a failure; it is an essential part of the journey to come to a deeper sense of wholeness. It is when we walk into the darkness of the self and come to the edge of what we know that we regain a true sense of self. Getting side-tracked in self-judgment does not help. It creates yet another distraction from the real task, which is to experience our fear, our pain, and to come to know it.

Being lost, or directionless, helped me understand what fear I had inside and the resistance to change, loss, and the unknown. At the moment that something makes sense, light illuminates. Imagine that something that you have run away from for so long is made clear to you, why it happened to you, and how you can move on from it. All these aspects of healing released the pain in me and freed energy for a much higher purpose. The power of understanding helps to create us and is paramount in healing. I observed that letting go would come when I had understood the process and myself.

Purpose and personal teachings come to us when we walk into the darkness. This challenge and all that it brings up is an opportunity to realise that we are much more than what we believe we are.

Moving past the borders within, delivers a strong self-belief and integrity. We learn that we are our greatest teachers. To walk with fear into the unknown is to let it take you by the hand and show you what lies beyond it.

I became empowered knowing that we can all be helped to come to the edge of our fear and go beyond it, but it must be our choice to step into the darkness. Sometimes, the edge is as far as we can go, and moving past it takes time. To use force is unhelpful and unnecessary in the healing process, and we can only move through fear and pain when we feel ready.

Some may need years of preparation before they can do so, and others can embrace it. Regardless of when we do it, not losing sight of this process is essential to empowerment.

Pain is Pain

"To ignore discomfort is reinforced all
around us, to get on, to stop making a fuss,
to not be weak. There is no doubt in my
knowledge and in my work that we have
made an enemy of feeling."

What never ceased to surprise me was how each time I went within and explored what I held; it would come with the same amount of intensity. I imagined it wouldn't. I believed that by consistently returning to release pain after pain, it would become an easier experience.

It is a natural reaction to feel uneasy in discomfort. I can imagine that you can think that because of what I do, and how I face pain, that I am in some way exempt from feeling too much. This is not true.

There was no doubt that recovery from the healing process was quicker, smoother, and easier the more I did it. I would come to the point that I was repeating the process of release daily, and it felt like I had grown etheric muscles in my arms, so I could carry myself through it. This was a real blessing, as I didn't feel overwhelmed or phased by the process anymore. But each time I would meet the pain, it was intense.

I somehow believed that just because I was becoming apt at meeting pain, it would feel easier the more I did it. This was not the case, pain is pain, and it hurts every time, which made me realise how beautiful and fragile human nature is.

I had come to know that this was not just my experience, but also the experience of those many people I had treated over the years.

When experiencing pain, or intense emotion, it feels intense and there is nothing we can do to dilute it.

I realised that I had a belief that empowerment meant losing this sense of fragility, vulnerability, and sensitivity. Collectively we have devalued these qualities, making them seem weak, unwanted, and unnecessary. To ignore discomfort is reinforced all around us, to get on, to stop making a fuss, to not be weak.

There is no doubt in my knowledge and in my work that we have made an enemy of feeling. Pain is pain, and it's uncomfortable, it hurts and it can feel at times like it devours you. But what the pain is showing us is that meeting our true self is a powerful experience, but one which we want to avoid. To cry, to allow myself to meet fear or sorrow, made me feel more human. What came after were the deepest sense of wholeness and the most real expression of my soul.

It became the most touching revelation for me that empowerment was at its core as gentle and as sensitive as a butterfly. It felt like the greatest illusion in life had been lifted from my soul, and that my empowerment laid in my humanness and sensitivity.

I would learn to see that my vulnerability, my sensitivity was the guiding light towards freeing all that was limiting me. I couldn't hide after knowing this.

The wish in my heart was to need for nothing, to know peace and love. I knew when I could experience the whole of me that my life would vibrate at a powerful level. I came to realise that sensitivity was key to knowing our higher potential. Opening the heart through healing develops our sensitivity. Releasing pain is an integral part of the path to raising our vibration.

I understood that without release, trapped fear and pain limits our growth. When we live making choices according to what our sensitivity reveals to us, we develop our higher potential and raise our energy to one that is full of life.

This self-inquiry and research proved to me that we are diluting the most powerful experience of the whole self by ignoring and suppressing feelings. I saw that I was living a sterile version of my potential because of my fear of pain.

We are used to the experience of ourselves functioning at a certain level and so changing it feels too much effort, too unfamiliar or too intense.

Life is powerful and yet we sidestep it every time we abandon ourselves by refusing to meet our fear and pain.

How to shift our consciousness so we can accept all processes within, without resistance or division, is of great significance for healing and empowerment.

The impact of resistance has created an internal culture of division. If we don't like something, we resist it, and prioritize what is agreeable over what is not. We don't want to feel bad, discomfort, or vulnerable, which is common to us all. We actively encourage a reality that supports suppressing and taking discomfort away at all costs, regardless of the implications of its impact on our soul development.

Whenever you find yourself saying, I sound stupid, this sounds strange, or I can't believe I'm saying this; these are all subtle ways that we avoid accepting our self. We sidestep what feels true to us to fit in and to not to stand apart.

~.~

By connecting to the inner self, our confidence increases. We regain confidence at a deeper level by renewing our sense of self-belief and worth through exploring vulnerability. We hide our sensitivity, seeing it as little value, or a sign of weakness.

Feeling what is inside of us allows us to become who we are, and not what we believe we should be. I remember not wanting to admit that I felt less than others, that my sensitivity made me feel different, unsure, and separate. Sharing with others this level of vulnerability was a hard road back to inner knowing. Even if we try to hide ourselves, the natural intelligence of how we heal within will eventually create the necessary circumstances to break this illusion of hiding.

The pain was my greatest teacher and spiritual mentor. Intensity is part of what makes us human, and feeling the world is our most natural state of being. I wish someone had told me this. That it was going to be my frailty, sensitivity, and vulnerability that was going to show me everything I needed to grow my being.

Pain is pain, no matter the level of evolution we are at, it is the leveller and sacred calibrator that open us up to a higher potential. The next time you feel pain, stop to meet it, be curious about it, and let yourself be led by it. It is life's intensity that awakens the possibility for growth at every level.

Inner Knowing

"I found an internal strength that needed no validation. I wanted to explore the true essence of me and the influence I have on shaping my reality."

Despite my very sensitive nature, inner knowing was still something I had to work consciously at growing. The task of altering consciousness does not happen quickly, it takes consistent practice to re-establish trust and to build up belief in one's true voice. I wanted to encourage my intuition at any opportunity, and so welcomed life's confusion. One way I would develop inner knowing was when I was at a crossroads in my life and I was unsure which path to take.

Firstly, I would prepare myself by relaxing, so the day's noise would leave me. I would use either breath work, tuning into the rhythm of my heart, or simply closing my eyes and centring myself in my physical body.

I became familiar with knowing when I had reached a deeper consciousness that was aligned with my inner sensitivity. I would then recall each path that lay ahead of me. I would imagine myself walking along one of the paths, which was not a forced or thought-based process, but more like dreaming. I would allow for any image or energy to surface once I had connected with that path.

When the energy of that path began to reveal itself to me, I would ask my higher self this question: is this path for me? Then I waited.

After repeating the question a few times, so that I could feel what was being asked, I would begin to sense the response through my whole being. This happened as a rising sensation in my body and heart. This could take the form of physical sensations like tingling in my body, pressure on my body, lightness, or tension. In the emotional body, I might feel joy, surrender, or feelings of being stuck or indifferent. I would wait and observe all of these responses.

Sure enough, after a little time, there would be a quality of energy that would show itself to me, if the choice was yes, this path was for me, and then it was often revealed through uplifting, freeing, and joyful feelings and sensations. If the answer was no, the energy was flat, sometimes low, or the sensation of being stuck. Each time I did this, my ability to intuit my response became clearer. I would then do the same with the other choice. I learned to trust this inner knowing and allow its wisdom to reveal itself to me.

~.~

When helping others to develop their connection to their heart self, I observed that it was rarely hard for anyone to connect with themselves in this way. Most were able to effortlessly follow the guidance and sense this higher knowing within them. However, what seemed to be the harder challenge was to trust this inner response and to follow it. Especially in the beginning, developing this inner connection, when following this intuitive response in the world, reason would try and take over, and doubt would follow.

When we try to understand the movement of this higher intelligence with the mind, we become lost trying to control or fixate on what we think should happen. If we only move from the mind, we cannot come close to our true Spirit.

The mind often strives for unobtainable, perfect conditions. Understanding ourselves as an integrated whole involves acknowledging all the dimensions of the self.

Inner knowing is based on a feeling that derives from a higher intelligence within. This movement is not based on reason, but on knowledge of one's highest good. This is why often, the answers that come through intuition are not what is expected, since expectation can block the development of our higher potential.

To have inner knowing is not the same as the desire to know what will come. What is true for us in this moment's experience cannot be based on a premeditated outcome. One flows and the other restricts.

To live a fulfilled and meaningful life comes when we align with our higher potential. This process teaches us to let go of thought-leading and instead, place our trust in the higher intelligence within.

By becoming aware of our true response to life, we flow with what we are and not with what we should be.

Our life is ever expansive and free. The connection to this force delivers us to our true state of being. It is this part of us that inner knowing is founded upon. The feeling is essential to developing our higher potential. When the heart is closed then inner knowing becomes buried too.

~.~

I began to realise that the foundation of me was based on an abundant life-giving energy. Being aligned with my inner knowing helped me to fill my life with what uplifted me. This was no longer based on an idealistic notion, but with direct experience of the abundant life force within me.

This higher intelligence showed me that I was only responsible for what came through me. I stopped worrying about what life was going to bring towards me, and I devoted myself to learning how to receive life-giving impulses in my daily life. This meant that I did things that felt like me, and not things that were based on thoughts or what others wanted of me.

I nurtured strength in me; bringing about sentiments that lifted me and helped create the world I wished for. I allowed my true self to reveal to me what I loved. I realised that when I filled my life with these sentiments,

I grew a powerful inner light and an unshakeable self-belief.

The power of inner knowing gave me self-confidence, which would govern the way I lived. I found an internal strength that needed no validation. I wanted to explore the true essence of me and the influence I have on shaping my reality. I realised that what I felt, thought, and believed in had a profound impact on what I was becoming. I began to steer myself in a vital and new way. My feelings and thoughts were me; they were the energy that created the movement of me and my world.

Creating my life based on information from the truest aspect of me created life-giving impulses.

My life became a co-creation and I realised that I stopped feeling separate from the world.

~.~

Inner knowing is formed from the subtle blend of the many aspects of us. All our senses are taking in messages that move us in one way or another. When someone has strong intuition, these messages are moved through the heart. When the heart is not open, intuition becomes distorted, and finding direction is confusing.

To grow inner knowing is to return to the heart centre, which informs us about what is meaningful, what lifts us, and what doesn't.

In the heart, we know what is real and what is not, no matter what is true for someone else.

Every person has a different path, and to follow what is unique in us is not some cliché, but an essential aspect of health, opening to our greater purpose and developing our higher potential.

By altering our consciousness, we become aware of ourselves and how we are responding to life. When we dull sensitivity and replace it with reasoning, we become distant from our true voice.

I am aware that even to ask you at this moment to recall what has genuinely touched you today may be harder than you think. This is because we often lead our life from the head and not from our feelings and intuition.

To find ways to support our inner knowing is part of the path of opening. To open is to question if what comes towards you in life resonates as true for you. Every choice we make either gives us life or holds us back. To sit on the fence of life is to not know what fulfils us. What is important is not to get lost in the fact that your way may not fit in with what others are doing, which does not help you. Being proactive in filling the heart with meaning grows inner knowing and light.

There is a belief that to follow the heart is an idealistic notion and a self-centred distraction.

For life to be lived to its full potential, we must break through this notion and see the power in our unique sensitivity.

Listening to the impulse of how you feel about things matters. What matters is to know that your sensitivity is ever-changing and informing you. You cannot project or expect what you will feel, for each moment is a new time. It is more about being present in the way you respond to life and following what is real for you.

God Within

"I wanted so much to have a teacher, a religion, a system that I could fit into, but the more I searched for it the further away I felt from feeling spiritual. "

I was always fascinated by spiritual discourse from any walk of life, whether religious, agnostic, mystic, or atheist. I welcomed any approach to help me open up my understanding of what was meant by spirituality. An aspect that would intrigue me were the teachings on the rules and practices of faith that help develop spiritual potential.

In popular teaching, it is believed that the seeker should follow one teacher or one system and remain with it to reach realisation. The essence of this teaching was also reflected in the practice of specific rites or rituals to develop the higher qualities to reach transcendence.

In my early exploration of spirituality, I wanted to respect age-old traditions. I wanted so much to have a teacher, a religion, a system that I could fit into, but the more I searched for it the further away I felt from feeling spiritual.

I was born into a Muslim family and faith, so I was able to understand how a consistent practice supported spiritual growth. I earnestly wanted to know how to free myself from limitations. I saw that some kind of discipline seemed essential. I had so much passion to know God, liberation, and realisation that I couldn't understand why I was not connecting with any religion or spiritual system.

Throughout my life I knew that I possessed an inner fire, which was aligned with my heart and at the core of my Spirit self. I knew that everyone else had this fire too, but I couldn't see it as strongly in others. Perhaps because of my awareness of my own inner fire, every system towards spiritual realisation felt limiting to me in some way. I would go so far and then realise that something fell short of truly freeing me.

I would have periods of my life where I took up a strong practice or discipline. I would meditate, do yoga, pranayama, read holy scriptures but I saw how much I would attach to the promise of its outcome. I wanted to acquire more peace, more connection, become closer to God, and so I made myself believe if I carried on, I could expect to be elevated. And so the pressure grew in me, what if I didn't practice? What if I didn't do it the right way? What if my heart didn't want to do it? I found I became more lost and confused by following another person's interpretation of spirituality.

The trust I had in my higher knowing gave me the awareness to discern whether what I was doing was there to empower me or not. I found that following a system or a discipline did not open me, but only compounded the need for control, restriction, or more expectations.

I became trapped in the idea of what a spiritual person should be; trying to be something I didn't feel. I felt like I knew what I was looking for but couldn't find it. I needed a path that was liberating and empowering, and which gave me the reins of myself so I could explore and evolve my spiritual path. It was as if I could already feel something inside of me that was inclusive, vital, and new.

I could feel the collective pressure, the judgment of others, who saw me as failing, and as less than those who were committed to a faith. It never ceased to surprise me how in every walk of life there is fear and judgment of difference. I wanted so much for the spiritual path, and those who were on it, to be exempt from creating further division, prejudice, and borders. I wanted them to reflect the fearlessness I had inside of me and to believe in a love that was inclusive, unconditional, and real.

So much emphasis is placed on promoting virtuous qualities that would make me feel ashamed or guilty that I was not as caring, as loving, or as pure as I should be. I was fed so many versions of what being spiritual looked like, and so I tried to force myself to be something that I wasn't.

I needed to find a way that was based on acceptance, and not fear, that reflected the wonder I felt in all of creation and who I was.

I believed that all of life was not something to resist and change but was there to understand.

~.~

As I grew the knowing in my heart, instead of forcing myself to do something when I became confused or disheartened, I listened to it. I gave what I was feeling value and let it reveal its truth to me. I observed that I was confused for a reason and that something didn't feel right for me. Instead of forcing myself to stay with a practice that didn't feel aligned with, I let go.

Overcoming the pressure of attachment to these practices was very difficult. The fear of what I might be losing if I didn't force myself to carry on felt so real. I desperately wanted to be free and to know God, but no outer path or practice was touching my heart.

I am not against practices that develop the qualities that support the opening of our spiritual path. I am speaking here about listening to the truth of the self. I placed these practices and disciplines above what I felt, and it was clear to me that it was taking something away from my sensitivity and not opening me up to love. When I heard a resounding "no" from my heart, I trusted it.

Living in a heart-centred way grew light in me that led me to discover that spirituality has no borders. To follow the wisdom of the self in the spiritual field is more feared than I realised.

I observed that when I became confused or disheartened on my spiritual path, it was because I was not resonating with it, and not because I was failing.

The practices that remained with me did so naturally, and those that fell away had done what they needed. I could not follow the way of forcing if my heart was not on board. Creation is endless in its unfolding, mysterious in its wake. I learned to trust that when one thing didn't fire me, then something else would.

There are many interpretations of spirituality and I found that following one system or one religion was not my truth. I overcame the collective prejudice and fear that can come from spiritual teachings that are not based on a single system. In time, the worry of what I felt I should think, say, or do, in a spiritual sense, left me.

Comparing myself and following others dulled the fire of my soul, and I came to believe that creation's truest path to enlightenment was through myself. I eventually realised that I needed to know the mystery of God through myself. After this realisation, I started to slow everything down, and to simply be with the mystery of myself, which is God. I saw that my heart was the closest teacher I had to God and to realisation.

Living a spiritual path is unique for everyone. No one has the same experience, regardless of which spiritual expression we follow, since the interpretation of its meaning is ours alone. I saw that any form of conformity bred control and was oppressive to expanding my being.

For me, a spiritual path gives life when it is integrated throughout the whole of our being, naked in its truth and unbound in its expression. If external acts of devotion cannot come from the heart, then they are meaningless.

To love is to feel all that one is and to continue to open the heart through oneself. Devotion cannot be faked and must come from the authentic feelings of our hearts, since the higher intelligence of life, God consciousness, which exists in everything, can easily read that which comes from our hearts. If what we call devotion does not come from the heart, then it does not have the capacity to open the higher consciousness within us.

Redefining Loneliness

"There lies much sorrow in having to leave the safety of the tribe and to walk in the wilderness alone. And so, we don't want it, we want to fit in and to follow. This is what makes turning inwards so hard. The further you go, the more alone you feel."

It makes absolute sense now that feeling lonely was an essential teaching to freeing my true spirit. But at the time it felt like a curse.

Those that knew me would often say how good I was with people. It was as if I couldn't be lonely, but the loneliness I was experiencing was something that I carried, no matter how sociable I was. I was not depressed, but I had a strong sense of feeling separate from the world.

Feeling disconnected from the world and from others granted me the space that gave rise to all the questions I had about life, the soul, and spirit. I didn't realise the deeper I moved towards integrating my higher self that feeling alone was part of the course.

The spiritual path asks us in some way to stand alone, or how I see it now, to stand apart. But standing apart is uncomfortable. I wanted to stay in the safety of the tribe, and not rock the boat. Things that are unfamiliar and confusing breed fear, and the primal instincts tell us on a subtle level to push away this threat.

A pressure within the collective does not encourage us to stand out from the crowd. We feel alienated, different, and marginalised when we do.

Regardless, if this is a primal instinct or not, the effect that it has on developing one's higher potential can feel demoralising.

Loneliness made me feel empty inside. This emptiness comes with the grief of having little to hold on to. Many have walked this path and know of the pitfalls. I didn't have a teacher, religion, or a system I followed. I allowed my heart to take me there and it did. Would a teacher have been useful? Would it have been easier to follow a system? All I know is that, for my heart, every step needed to feel real. I didn't see anything that felt like me outside, so I was forced to feel my way towards my true self.

~.~

My own direct experience, and helping others on their journey, helped me to understand the purpose of loneliness. To see our deepest fears and pain one must walk alone, another can stand by, but the direct experience is ours alone. The healing process revealed to me the true purpose of loneliness.

I witnessed that when people dared to break down, to feel their pain, to feel how lost they were, and how alone it made them feel, something incredible would follow. At the point of feeling most broken, something else would begin opening within the person's spirit.

It was in the ether where angels would gather overhead to witness, in awe of our courage and to bring the love to support our transformation. I would observe how beautiful a person's spirit was when it struggled in pain, searching for its freedom.

In terms of energy, this was an amazing thing to observe. In the alchemy of the moment, we surrender our heartache and longing, we surrender to life and something deep within our soul changes. At this moment we are offered hope. To come to this point of surrender, courage is required. It is essential to have the courage to move beyond fear and to face our pain, however, in the initial stage; we may feel a sense of shock that tries to numb us from facing the pain. As we move through the fear, courage is not experienced in a conscious way, but often only realised once we have faced the pain.

When we struggle, and are in the process of releasing, very little feels right, and it is painful. But it is when we break down in tears, when we are crying out for help that we clear the way of the heart. It's when we have the courage to free the pain and to meet ourselves in pain, that we come closer to our true essence, and in turn, grow the intimacy and love that we have towards ourselves.

I learned that the feeling of separation and disconnection from life is, at some level, a universal struggle. It was when separation started to dissolve, and love was unfolding within me that I began to release the state of loneliness.

~.~

We get used to endless distractions, information, and influences from the outside world and we become very full. This brings a false sense of security that we are part of something. There lies much sorrow in having to leave the safety of the tribe and to walk in the wilderness alone. And so, we don't want it, we want to fit in and to follow. This is what makes turning inwards so hard. The further you go, the more alone you feel.

I can't remember the exact day that loneliness left me, but I do remember what it taught me. The higher path is asking us to break through the illusion that we are alone, separate, and disconnected, and until we do it, the illusion will remain. A fountain of love resides within each of us and is the cornerstone of our existence. Loneliness reminded me that I still had more questions to ask before I found my way home.

In truth, there is no map, manual, or script to develop our spiritual potential. Each of us stands alone in the great mystery of our self and our relationship to all of creation is ever-changing and unfolding. The challenge is to experience the struggle of life and to open one's heart despite it. By living a heart-centred life, I was able to live through loneliness and not fear it. I came to learn that the inner world was as vast as the universe, and when I had freed all that weighed me down, I lived interconnected with all of life, a state where only peace remains, and life is lived without effort.

Love

"Love is powerful, and to have love we must be empowered to be able to hold it... Love is intrinsic to being, and not something we need to acquire; it has always been there, behind the many layers that mask our true essence. To come to it and be it, we have to learn how to peel away the many layers that keep us apart."

After practicing for many years healing myself and others, as well as teaching about how to develop one's inner knowing, I had reached a level of empowerment that freed my heart and allowed me to ask for anything I wished for. I longed to know the deepest love. At the time, I'm not sure what I imagined I was asking for, but I needed to know unconditional love and to understand what self-love meant.

I wanted to know a love that was not sentimental, but pure and unconditional, which I could hold within throughout my entire life. The love I was asking to know was about the intimacy of life, and about surrendering to this love. I wanted to feel what it was like to be love, rather than falling in and out of love, but simply to be with it without holding back on loving.

It is still difficult for me to comprehend that to experience true love; there is no attachment to anything. The version of love that I and most people know is the one that holds on to others, situations, and experiences. This kind of love is conditional and differs from unconditional love, which holds no value for itself nor believes itself to be higher or lesser than anything.

I found out that my yearning for love was a mirror for a much higher calling, which was to be free. For me, freedom did not mean success, material, or psychological gain, but in being liberated from all that holds us back from being in the true state of love. To know this deepest form of love was to know my true spirit.

~.~

I remember when I was in my twenties I found this love. I was doing a meditation that I had developed after being introduced to energy work. I would sit and feel the energy in my hands, heart, and higher self. I did it every day because I loved to play with energy and not for one moment did I expect anything from it.

Because of my innocence and deep curiosity, it would reveal to me the greatest love of all. I experienced an opening or awakening that was a state of euphoria. It was so profound that the love I experienced in this state was too much, too powerful for me to hold.

After each time it happened, I would go back to my everyday life and feel a divine energy reaching out through me to others, sharing its love with everyone. It was so profound that I felt I didn't know what was happening.

The most extraordinary feeling I had was being able to sit with the pain and suffering of everyone around me and only feel love in it. I felt no sorrow, but a kind of celebration of life, no matter whether it was full of pain, sorrow, or joy. This love knew nothing but the celebration of life, and accepted everything as the expression of God, loving it no matter what.

The healing power of love is unmistakable; it can transform any pain since it is painless. I came to see that love is not bound by anyone's rules, since it is free. Love has no relation to selfishness, compromise, or expected virtues, and there is no apology or need for validation. This is not a self-centred expression, but compassionate and connected.

During this time, I believed that I had glimpsed God, and felt the glory of creation, but because of my pain, I could not be in this euphoric state for very long. Each time I entered into that state, a part of me became scared of feeling so much love. There was so much fear inside of me challenging this love. I felt I didn't deserve it, and that I wasn't worth this level of intimacy with life, with God.

I was young at the time and had no sense of who I was without pain. Suddenly, coming to know this state of love was not easy since it brought all my pain to the surface, and I felt I couldn't stay there. I decided to close the door and not to return there again.

The brightness of love can feel like the greatest burden when one's whole sense of self is not free. Discord prevents this level of love from really expressing itself. Fear holds it back. To know this level of love and to live without borders needs courage and commitment. And so, it would take me another twenty years before I felt worthy enough to open the door. This time I was ready, and with all of my heart I asked to know the highest and deepest love again.

I had learned that voicing my longing was a very important part of manifesting. It did not necessarily need to be told to a person, but life needed to hear it in some way. To bring about something I wanted, life needed to read it through the sentiments of my heart.

You might think this is an easy thing to bring about, but then why do so many people not receive what they want? The reason has to do with the heart. You see, we cannot cheat life, for intention to be potent; it needs to be expressed from the heart. Therefore, when I feel something that I long for from the heart, then I offer something strong to the manifesting process.

What I didn't know was how it would come, or what I needed to do to get there.

By asking life for what we want, we can't know how long the journey will be, or what form it will take, since this path has no fixed rules. But what we do know is that if we continue to remember it, it will come.

~.~

It's hard to put into words the feeling of interconnectedness that inner love brings. We are so used to feeling an outer love, to love someone or something. We can all live this higher state of love, but something I realised on my path was that we have to feel worthy of this level of love.

We all seek love, one way or another. We have an innate knowing when we are receiving love, and when we don't, which is felt the strongest in our childhood. As we grow, and as our pain and insecurities sometimes overwhelm us, then love becomes something else.

It was a struggle for me to receive a higher love when I was younger because pain blocks the way of the heart. It's not as simple as saying "love me" and I will feel love. What we carry as pain, fear, and suffering must be freed to know a higher love. Unworthiness ties us to experiencing only a limited version of love. The more love we feel the greater the experience we have of ourselves and all that we carry.

Love is powerful, and to have love we must be empowered to be able to hold it.

To equate love with empowerment is not the most widely interpreted version. Love is intrinsic to being, and not something we need to acquire; it has always been there, behind the many layers that mask our true essence. To come to it and be it, we have to learn how to peel away the many layers that keep us apart.

Prayer

When there is a prayer in each one's heart,
life will free itself and open to the splendour
of its greatness.

Beyond all time will life become
and a great peace will fall on the
earth.

Blessed be all beings. In the name of the
Holy One within each of us this truth is
given.

Teachings

Each truth can be a daily meditation, prayer, or reminder of the path to realise oneself. It may resonate with you at different times of your life, and ultimately help you. This is a voice that believes in you and is a reminder that when you feel lost to look within, for all understanding lies in you.

~.~

The Highest Good

To ignite intrigue for the higher life,
you first light that which lies within you.

-

In life is the opportunity to embrace yourself,
to learn about your nature and to create out of
your higher potential into the physical world.

-

To live the higher reality is to return home, to align
to your truth and to weave with the pattern of life
and not against it.

-

Your innate self never forgets the brightness you
hold, which lives in the highest sense of you and asks
for your truth to be realised.

-

In the higher realm nothing masks your essence and
you are able to express your true purpose.

-

To open to your higher state, your fragile nature must
be seen.

-

To live carefully is to become conscious and aware of
what you are becoming.

-

In sensitivity, feelings show you the way to the
highest good.

-

To experience the tenderness of love you are asked to
express all the colours of you without limitation.

-

The call is to challenge all that is not in line with your
sensitivity, where your higher sense of self resides.

-

Without feeling there can be no honour to the higher
self. Through feeling one finds realness and brings
that which is true alive.

-

With a free heart the prayer to grow light is clear.
Through the sentiments in the heart reality can be
transformed for the highest good.

-

Seeing all the shades of you, you learn how to re-
create reality to serve your higher potential, which is
free and whole, for in wholeness you have the
potential to radiate magnificent colours.

-

The true self cannot be known through the external
reality alone. The fullness of you has to be lived in
truth with the creative life force within, where you
transform your outer reality for the highest good.

-

Love is let in when you allow the power of the
creative force to lead you and trust its guidance. You
need only trust this inner guidance to realise your
higher potential.

Truth: Part One

The cream of life, the fullness of being, comes from emersion in your inner world. To be given that crowning, you must stay true to exploring what is true for you, beyond all other external influences.

-

In every layer of you, truth can be revealed.
This is the flowering of the soul, where the
loving heart is in full bloom.

-

Learning how to experience the true self
opens the doorway to changing reality.

-

To create the self is to become conscious
and aware of all that you are, and of that
which drives you. Being able to show who
you are makes the will and the heart stronger.

-

In reclaiming the true self, light is allowed to lead.
From this point life has the potential to become
simple and uncomplicated.

-

When your truth emanates into the world an
invincible faith is created, since this is what lies
in you.

To not hide your struggle is to shine in a higher state
of being.

-

To be vulnerable is to see what is real and to
experience all that it is showing you. When faced with
the realness of being it can feel intense, since it comes
with the power of truth.

-

Care is needed for you to remember to find space,
so that tenderness can exist. By showing feelings,
and to be all that you are, without censorship,
belief in truth can exist.

-

One's true self has to be a direct experience to know
it is real.

-

Self-realisation is waking to the higher self of being;
this cannot be premeditated, or given to you by
another, but is yours to see directly.

-

Courage is needed to explore the self and master what
is real.

-

All that touches the heart remains as your
everlasting truth.

Truth: Part Two

Pain is a mighty teacher, the holder of truth and all that is real.

-

To move past pain is to open to what you feel, the doubts, the struggle and the fears.

-

Important messages are communicated to you when you seek to understand pain.

-

By facing pain and understanding the original wound, truth is released and the higher learning that the soul needs, becomes integrated.

-

Pain invokes courage and so strengthens the will of being to face that which takes you to the brink of what you know.

-

The healing process involves the understanding of the unease of life and how you became caught in struggle.

What waits in you is light, for truth is always there
where shame does not exist.

-

In the true self there is no guilt, shame or regret,
for no part of you is a mistake.

-

To walk with fear is to befriend it, hold it in high
esteem for your truth is waiting to be realised.

-

In every fear faced you bring the release of higher
teachings for soul growth. This is permanent and
sustaining.

-

When the heart feels broken, it is not, in truth it is
you opening through the expansion of yourself.

-

When grief comes, it is creation's way to lift you from
the monotony of your life and to realign you with
what feels real to you.

-

The joy of living comes about from truth, for it is
truth that leads you to the path of purpose.

One has become a guest to their truth, strangers to
their light.

-

The higher task is to live one's inner reality fully
without borders to truth.

Deliver This

What lies in the heart is to be cherished. Love begins
by speaking to you through the heart, the place of
courage where the light of the creator resides.

-

You know what to believe in and what not to, what
the right path is and what is not for you. Follow in life
what matters to you, since what is meaningful comes
from the impulses of the heart.

-

The heart explores its surroundings for the purpose
of connection, exploration and experience. It is able
to intuit and to be touched by the world around it.

-

To open to what lies in the heart is to accept both
sorrow and joy alike, since you cannot favour one
over the other in order to grow.

-

To create out of the higher fire is to surrender and
give value to the inner processes that make you feel
vulnerable. In this you train yourself to live from
the heart.

The journey to the light is to forgive yourself that fear
is in you.

-

Showing is essential for personal care to exist in the
world. To realise this, you walk naked and speak
truth, even when you feel alienated. The innate being
that is you wants to become all that it needs to be.

-

Hope is cast from self-belief, since you know how to
deliver yourself to the dream of what you came for.

-

The task is not to suppress or run away from the
intensity of emotion that is now longing to be heard
in the heart.

-

Life becomes careless when the heart is made an
enemy of.

-

To walk this path, go slowly.

-

When you go slowly you listen to the inner self, since
this is what is yearning to be balanced. This is prayer.
When you are able to listen to what is true for you
then this delivers light.

-

When you become visible to the world, then love
comes in.

The Power Within: Part One

In not forgetting yourself gives access to an invincible
power of will that can cast a light that banishes all
doubt.

-

What is real for you creates a strong energy and is
clear in the world. In the sovereignty of being one
does not have to be anything they
believe they should be.

-

You have the ability to know all that you are, since
you are the keeper of yourself. The higher wish is to
create out of power within and to drive this dream.

-

What you came to do for your higher self is to
unburden your being of all that makes you heavy, to
grow your innate power and to be all that you can be.

-

Life calls you to feel abundance again, to fear nothing
and to embrace the fountain of power within you.
Love waits for you when you are ready to open to all
that you are.

-

Your will is the driving force behind what you express
to the world and forms and shapes the reality you
wish for.

-

Emotions and thoughts are powerful, and affect you
on a profound level, since they are the reality you live.

-

The real aspect of you is fearless, where all doubts
are answered.

-

The way of empowerment is to make yourself visible.
To live with tenderness all parts of you are accepted
and all welcomed.

-

In one's fall there is the potential for the brightness
within to be illuminated.

-

What lies beyond the noise of the soul is an impenetrable force, the resounding presence of oneness.

-

Trusting your higher sensitivity is to witness the true power of life. It cannot be rushed, for this is where true joy and peace reside.

The Power Within:
Part Two

Your way of seeing is powerful.

-

The mind is a powerful ally and when harnessed
freedom can exist.

-

For empowerment, one trains the mind to be in
relationship with the heart. When aligned with the
heart, the mind is free to serve what you believe.

-

What creates reality comes from your intention and
what you believe in.

-

With a strong sense of self, you have the ability to
create the outer reality that you wish for.

-

When the world that you create comes from inner knowing, then you can live with power without.

-

The creative force moves freely through the spheres of love in the heart and this alchemy provides a powerful, sustaining force.

-

The inner life has the potential to provide you with everything you need to have a fulfilling and peaceful life.

-

When life is lived in the complete self then you are not lost. You feel the strength of knowing that all is one.

-

What may seem empty within is concealing the force of the creative fire. You live the inner fire when you are free from the ties that hold you back.

-

Empowerment comes when you are complete within.

-

True power lies in the vastness of a free state of being.

Surrender

In healing, the seeds of hope are planted.

-

You are learning not to fight but to surrender to yourself. Through the acceptance of pain you can start to learn the higher teachings of why pain has come, and what you need to learn from it.

-

Willingness to face personal struggle and surrender to it, opens you to the higher potential.

-

No one can give you sovereignty. To be the authority of yourself must come from you. To be the creator of your life comes from witnessing the core of who you are. This comes from the conscious choice to surrender and accept yourself.

-

To allow the wisdom of you to lead, you must gain trust in the inner world. Here lies freedom and the belief in a higher potential.

-

To have wisdom you must break free from the safety
of what you know and expect. Trusting the wisdom
of emotion is key to your higher potential, for creative
awakening is led by what you feel.

-

Going beyond what is known to you unlocks your
higher potential. You come into life for this purpose,
to create the self whole again.

-

You have not been given an impossible task, since
you have evolved to this point and possess all you
need to face the fears inside of you.

-

Self-belief is a hard path to follow if you look outside
of yourself for it.

-

Many fear the expectation of emptiness if they go
within, but this is far from what flows through this
sacred place of knowing.

-

Through the essence of the heart force one brings the
courage to accept all that they feel. This expression is
not a premeditated, prepared or formulated act but
rather it is vital, new and resonates from hope.

-

Learning about all that you are is a higher prayer.

Governance:
Part One

Light is indefinite in character, ever-changing and
ever-growing. Everything is becoming in life, moving
in the way it is designed to. The call is to know what
is within you, to be conscious of what you
have become and are creating in life.

-

Purpose lies in the maturity of your light, which is the
pride of existence, where you integrate the higher self
into life.

-

To experience the infinite parts of you,
one moves through the heart force.

-

Look to both what is pleasurable and what is painful
and accept all expressions as essential to what you are
now.

-

Everyone is creating, and what you are creating is in your hands. To not forget and to strengthen the will of yourself moves you to brightness.

-

In the wisdom of life, you are given all that you need to complete yourself.

-

What is true from the heart is pure in intention and will seek to be shared, for there are no shadows created from it. From this you are led.

-

What is worth carrying begins in the heart.

-

In each moment of life there is the choice to respond in one way or another, to seek one thing over another. That which you give attention to affects the reality you create, and that which you are becoming.

-

To cultivate what feels right, you first need to observe what feels wrong.

-

You are not the passenger in your life, you are the driving force. To master yourself within you have to take the reins of your life.

Governance:

Part Two

To return to wholeness and regain self-belief, healing
for the soul must happen on all levels of being. The
potential to hear the call of your true voice comes in
the darkest hour.

-

For balance you must address imbalance. Living
carefully is the awareness of this fragile process and
supporting your natural flow towards harmony.

-

The task is to remove the blocks to your own
brilliance. From here reality is transformed according
to a balanced and natural order.

-

By understanding the nature of pain you can be
helped to move past the need to escape it.

-

Pain is a signpost when there is a need to resolve something within that is waiting to be healed. It does this by bringing about a heightened awareness and this may make you feel uncomfortable.

-

The discomfort is absolutely necessary for it is trying to get your attention.

-

The discomfort created by pain lifts you out of a 'normal' state of being and sharpens the senses.

-

Blocked energies manifest as pain.

-

To be in optimum health the energy force within must flow freely. The release of emotion is the flow that frees the heart.

-

All energies created want to expand and grow whether positive or negative in nature.

-

When life's processes of struggle and healing present themselves, you are forced to the core of yourself.

-

-

The experience of living in extreme internal conditions facilitates awakening. It is the shadow parts of yourself that are doorways to return to light.

-

Suffering is not caused by the existence of pain but by the fear of facing it.

The Greater Good

In each choice there lies the opportunity to create a
lighter world for the good of all.

-

When you touch love, with its giving nature, and
witness that which is in alignment with the greater
good, you bring peace.

-

The fight is not between each other but to face fear
and to live your personal truth.

-

The potential to create paradise on earth is unfolding
in life all the time. To return to the state of
completion is to achieve eternal joy, which
is the higher longing.

-

The essence of love cannot be reasoned; it must be
felt and so cannot be reached through the mind alone.
To feel the world from the heart is to know care.

-

That which opens the self is found in higher
sensitivity within.

-

Through the interconnectedness of yourself, you
create the world you wish to live in.

-

The cradle of life lays in the tender essence, that
which is the heart in its pure form. To know this level
of tenderness provides the incentive to live our lives
with the upmost care. Through this realisation, is life
overflowing and abundant in nature.

-

The stream of life that created the earth knows the
sovereignty of its creation. What lives from this truth
unfolds through the interconnectedness of all life.

-

Hope is infectious since very few carry this light.
What you do affects everything and everyone. Being
in the light is the gift of heaven on earth. When you
feel your light is strong you can't help but release this
to all those around you.

-

To want to expand is a perpetual and natural process. In the brilliance of your shining you affect the reality of those around you. The higher wish is the return to the core of being.

-

We can help each other to become visible and promote the sentient parts of ourselves.

-

To create through light comes when we know our inner light, and in so doing we are able to see light in the world.

The Holy

All is hallowed, clear and justified.
This is the intimacy of life.

-

The Holy lives within, without and in all of existence.
When this matrimony awakens, there can only be
eternal peace.

-

To awaken that which is Holy comes from a higher
sensitivity of being. To open is to re-learn to trust
yourself and awaken this potential. This is the
knowing of love within.

-

The calling of your heart will show you back to
wholeness. Your being naturally reaches towards
oneness and wholeness, since this is what it knows.

-

The potential of life is profound, for your natural
intelligence will seek its way to higher ground and
intuitively knows its way back.

Cultivating life from the heart is to be in direct connection to the eternal self, so that the divine can express its blessing.

-

Believing that the supersensitive world is out of reach creates many images of what is Holy but its true expression comes from inner knowing.

-

When vulnerable you become heightened and come closer to the potential of hearing the true voice that leads you to the Holy within.

-

All have the potential to achieve oneness. It is not merely for the gifted or elite, it is achievable by all and this potential waits in you if you wish it.

-

When you steer destiny, the light in life becomes vast, since you live in a state of shining. There is the potential in you to reach the Holy beyond pain and to forgive yourself. By going within comes the potential to go higher.

-

What is most valuable in life is to succeed in creating yourself and to find your way to the sacred within.

-

What lies inside you matters.

-

What has been will be again.

Inner Work

Eight transformational and progressive steps

to healing the self and developing

higher consciousness

~.~

The path to wholeness and completion relies on the conscious efforts of inner work. To become whole, purposeful, and empowered we must align to the truth that flows through us. The pressing task of moving beyond the borders of the self is critical in remedying soul crises.

Connection flourishes when we make connection within ourselves. Pain and discord are signs of when we have held ourselves back and compromised our truth. Life cannot expand where intolerance exists. The inner wisdom of the true self is the guiding light towards realisation.

The following 'Eight Steps' are processes that heal the self and develop higher consciousness. Each one is designed to open dimensions of the self that are vital aspects to recovering the true self. One is learning a new way of seeing based on truth in the self.

Move through each step in the order that they are delivered. As the connection deepens within, use these practices and knowledge in your way.

Step One:

Awakening the Heart

When one is in touch with the sensitivity of the heart, then inner knowing can develop. Without the heart intact we struggle to know ourselves and become who we are designed to be. The heart interconnects our knowing with higher consciousness and greater purpose of oneself. To deepen connection in our outer world happens when the connection to our heart is strong.

The following step will grow the tender connection to your heart and develop the foundation for inner knowing.

Take Action:
This step can be performed anywhere as long as you have no distractions and interruptions. It can be as short as a few minutes or as long as you wish.

Close your eyes and take 4 few deep breaths. Begin by placing the palm of your hands on your heart. Observe the rise and fall of the chest and stay there until you start to feel yourself relax. As the connection to the chest area deepens notice if you can feel the heart beating. Your attention will come and go this is natural. If your mind wanders bring your attention back to the rise and fall of the chest and the heartbeat.

After a few moments recall a loving memory, a person or animal you love, or any experience that you felt deep love. Stay with the memory or person, allow for the feelings of love you have to fill your heart, and continue to observe this feeling in the chest area. Stay longer with the feeling and imagine spreading this loving warmth to the rest of your body. Allow the energy to move through the whole body and imagine expanding this out into the world.

The more you focus on this practice, the more the sentiments of love in the heart will fill your being. Your aim is to receive and allow the heart force to penetrate deep within. Relax and enjoy this healing energy until you feel you are ready to come back.

When you are ready, leave your inner space by becoming conscious of the outer world. Hear the sounds around you and slowly start to stretch the body and open your eyes. Take a few moments to be aware of how this practice has made you feel.

What you have connected to is the power of your heart. Each time you visit this space and practise you will bring the sentiments of your heart into consciousness. You are providing life-giving energy to all dimensions of yourself. Here lies the beginning of creating a clear path to your heart.

Practise this daily and you will start to feel a change in the way you connect to your inner world. This change comes in many ways, a deeper wholeness in yourself, more gratitude in your life, a freer expression of yourself, or greater clarity of how you feel. In this simple practice you can begin to see powerful shifts in your life.

Step Two:

Connecting

What you give attention to creates your reality. When we consistently turn our gaze outwards, we rely on external influences to create ourselves. Inner truth moves from the heart and no one else has your heart. To bring a deeper sense of connection into our lives begins with this simple step.

Take Action:

Make time for daily introspection. Begin by taking 10 minutes out of your day, whether by going for a walk, sitting in a quiet space, or simply closing your eyes. Before you start, make a point of pausing and becoming aware of the body. You are stopping the flow of your day and preparing your senses for this task. Allow yourself to observe any rising sensations or tensions in the body. Shifting your gaze to the body helps you start to shift your consciousness. After a few minutes of tuning in ask this question:

'How do I feel?'

Repeat this question quietly and slowly but say it out loud.

Do not try to answer this with your mind but observe what happens to your gaze when you do this. Remain only with this question and observe what arises in you. The aim is not to get anywhere training yourself to get used to turning your attention inwards is what matters. Notice as you go in what you start to feel or think.

This level of self-awareness is often harder to do than we think. Allowing space to check in with yourself can break through the barrier between you and your authentic self. With this simple question you are able to go within and remind yourself that what you feel matters.

Step Three:

Self Care

Inner work can impact us on all levels. Subconsciously we carry stories within that can anchor deep into the heart and become part of us. Even if they hold us back and do not serve us, letting the stories go can be challenging. Loss and sorrow play a significant role in the healing journey. Often we close our hearts to protect ourselves from feeling vulnerable. For this reason, reconnecting to inner sensitivity and the healing process needs a whole-centred approach. Self-care is a vital step to succeeding in returning to the true self.

When we feel discomfort and vulnerable, we are often are unaware of what we need to help support us. Therefore, allowing ourselves to open again must be a careful task. Learning how to self-soothe through our experiences establishes a safe holding ground. Even if we feel we don't need it our inner child does.

Take Action:

Before Practices...

Give yourself enough time and space. Feeling you have to rush places pressure on you to perform.

Let go of your expectations. If it feels like you are not experiencing a lot don't worry and carry on. Remind yourself that this process comes in many ways and comparing yourself with an idea of what it should be like only stifles your process.

Feel secure and safe in the space you choose to do your practice. Knowing you will not be disrupted helps you remain in your inner world.

Be observant when you feel you are forcing something to happen. Often, we may feel rushed, or the timing is not right. If you feel too tired, stressed, or pressured don't force yourself to practise. We serve ourselves in a greater way by listening to what we need and this may be to rest. When you feel more in balance you can try again.

Preparing before a practice can enrich your experience and helps give a feeling of being held as you dive within. You can choose one or more of the following to do or add something that you already do to help you alter consciousness and feel into your higher self.

Light an incense stick or resin as this calms the mind and body.

Place your palms together and close your eyes. Remain here as long as you need. This popular prayer position forms an energetic circuit in the body and calms the senses quickly.

Burn aromatherapy oil that helps soothes the nervous system.

Listen to quiet and gentle music that relaxes mind and body.

After Practices…

Feeling out of balance shortly after a release is natural. You are not aiming to avoid this. An essential part of reconnecting and learning how to govern the self is learning how to integrate discomfort. If you feel ungrounded, highly sensitive, or anxious after doing a practice, any one of the following will help bring balance.

Lie down on the floor. Sensing the spine connected to the earth take 4 long and slow deep breaths. Stay here as long as you need as this has a soothing effect on the nervous system and will ground you.

Any form of gentle exercise will help move the energies and balance you. If you have a limited time, even five minutes will help. You can walk, run, cycle, or do yoga. Movement is a great healer for calming the mind, bringing us into our bodies, and releasing beneficial chemicals associated with feeling happy and confident.

As you start to grow inner connection it is helpful to incorporate more time for introspection and rest. If you experience intense releases or internal struggle don't be afraid to take time out of your normal routine to do and plan nothing. Reflection and making space is a powerful way of allowing you to recharge and find peace in the stillness.

Make time for simple activities that help calm you and encourage repetitive actions that are familiar such as gardening, walking, gentle exercise, playing games, or reading. Going back to basics is soothing and gives space to assimilate deeper processes.

Develop healthy eating habits when starting to open and release. Nutritious pure juice drinks are very effective in giving extra nourishment to the body. The whole of one's being can be challenged through discomfort and the healing process and uses up much energy that is needed during emotional release and rebalancing. Give yourself a soothing health drink or herbal tea is harmonising and replenishes the body.

Step Four:

Develop Inner Knowing

Inner knowing is what differentiates everyone from each other. It is the expression of our unique design that delivers the knowledge of what we are here for. The loss of inner knowing has created profound levels of disconnect and mistrust within ourselves, each other and the world.

The following practice builds on inner sensitivity and will help tune you into your knowing. Every dimension of you from the physical, emotional, mental and spiritual planes is interconnected and functions as one. The aim is to encourage the wisdom of the whole self to shine through.

Take Action:

If you feel you are still new to developing inner connection give yourself around 20 minutes to practice this technique. Those who feel more adept may only need half this time. Do this practice sitting down as lying on the floor can make you feel sleepy and this practice needs your attention.

Firstly, repeat awakening the heart in Step One.

As you begin to feel the heart force fill your body remain here for a few minutes taking in the loving energy. When you are ready, recall any issue that you are having in your life. It may be a decision you are worried about making, whether to make a change in your life or whether you want to be with someone or not. You can bring anything that concerns you and you want more clarity.

Whatever it is, create a question that you can ask that summarises your concern. It could be, Am I making the right choice? Should I go for this job? Is this person good for me? Start by articulating your worry out loud as if addressing it to your heart. Describe how you feel about it, why it worries you and your wish to resolve it. This helps orientate you about your issue.

As you hear yourself describe the issue the question to ask may become clear.

When you have the question you want to answer say it out loud and repeat this several times slowly. Then wait.

Over the next 5-10 minutes observe the response at every level of yourself. The following guidelines can help orientate your attention.

Notice if physically you feel any sensations or impulses, does your energy feel light or heavy, do any emotions arise, do you feel pressure and if so how, do you feel relaxed, are you tensing, does your energy feel uplifted, at peace, and so on.

Take your time. When observing these responses you are learning to sense if you are experiencing uplifting and life-giving impulses. If what you observe makes you feel empowered and free this is a positive response to your question. If you feel held back, pressured, or your energy is low, this is your whole self showing you to choose another direction. You may receive messages or see visions in this space and this is another way that your wisdom reveals itself to you. Learning to follow that which empowers and lifts the whole of you moves you in the right direction.

Close the space by placing the palm of your hands together. Give thanks to the higher intelligence in you and feel the peace of this energy-balancing position. You can come back to this practice with the same or other questions as many times as you need.

This practice needs performing regularly to grow inner-connection, confidence, and belief in what you feel. Courage is needed to explore the self, master what is real, and follow it.

Step Five:

Empower Vulnerability

When a child hurts we tend to them, offer our attention, and are with them to ease their pain. This is essential to develop the human bond and grow inner strength through adversity. Without this, we breed rejection, hardship, and intolerance within the soul. This process is also necessary for us to grow trust, fortitude, and strength within.

Allowing one's vulnerability to be an accepted part of life can bring enormous change to carrying the self through adversity. One's vulnerability is not a weakness but a tenderness that carries strength. To renew belief in oneself is to explore one's vulnerability. To feel unsafe can unearth intense emotions of unworthiness, failure, guilt, shame, or not being good enough. To ignore these feelings we create further discord, distortion, and disharmony.

Continuing to escape the feelings of vulnerability holds us back from our potential. We are learning to overcome the intolerance that we have created towards parts of ourselves and transcend a punishing reality. This step helps validate the self and grow the inner strength we need to be with every shade and expression within.

Take Action:

Take a quiet moment at the end of your day to be aware of whether over the day you experienced feeling grief, guilt, shame, unworthiness, fear, anxiety, insecurity, or helplessness.

The most helpful time for this is just before sleep. Place the palm of your hands together and let your mind wander through the day's experiences. If you remember a vulnerable feeling allow it to surface and introduce the following message, tell yourself,

'It is not wrong to feel helpless, unsure, or out of control. I am a sentient being, created to feel everything without borders. To feel unsure is part of opening. From this feeling I am reminded to place my trust and faith in the higher intelligence of the true self.'

Repeat this several times until you naturally feel ready to stop. To finish, place your hands on the heart for a few minutes and feel its nurturing rhythm. If at this point you feel discomfort within then do 'Step One: Awakening the Heart' to help bring further reassurance and balance.

Noticing change within can take a few weeks or months with regular practice. When you feel more confident and more accepting of your process, you are ready to implement the following step.

Step Six:

Grow Sensitivity

If you have reached this point you will have started feeling deeper into the dimensions of yourself. Taking responsibility for how far you go is important for your well-being. Wanting to escape inner pain and discomfort has become deeply ingrained in the psyche but also keeps us feeling safe. We naturally move away automatically from what makes us feel insecure and vulnerable.

The purpose of inner work is to re-establish the connection to one's inner sensitivity and higher potential. We can help change the tide of helplessness and disempowerment within. We are transforming the debilitating response to vulnerability into an empowering and life-giving process of acceptance, self-care, and release.

When opening, you choose to go there at the pace that is right for you. These practices are designed to open you safely and the following is invaluable information to be aware of.

If during practice you experience intense feelings you cannot manage, pause or stop. Either go back to using a previous practice or take a break for a few days and try again.

If you have experience of past trauma, mental health issues, abuse, or shock then approach this practice with care. The human spirit is strong yet we must possess enough inner light to navigate intense emotion. Releasing intense experiences will heal you and return your power. Go far as you can and if it feels too much, reach out and seek professional help. To bury your pain only blocks your truth and limits you.

Do not underestimate the power of release through your tears. The act of crying offers an alchemical response within the whole of being and aligns us again to who we are. Many imagine that crying is pointless, a waste of time, and brings nothing to help. In a world that makes an enemy of feelings, one can feel ashamed of crying. We do not fail or grow weaker through our tears. It is a transformational process that unburdens the heart and allows life to be moved by our truth. With every tear the truth of our soul is laid bare and this becomes the prayer in the heart.

In a world where we want to gain instant results, we speed through processes. What you carry within does not adhere to these rules. One must let go of the need to tick a box and get somewhere. What you need will come to you but in a way that is right for you. Let go of expectations. Continue to hold yourself with compassion.

Take Action:
This practice needs a period of at least 20 minutes or longer if you need it. Prepare to have no distractions and find a space alone where you feel relaxed. This space can take any form as what you need is not necessarily like another.

Take a few minutes to acclimatise yourself to the space you are in. If you are in nature you can take a walk, sit, and take in the environment. If you are in a confined space, take four deeper breaths, close your eyes, and let your mind wander without forcing anything. To prepare, repeat awakening the heart in 'Step One'. Consider implementing any of the self-care points in 'Step Three'.

When relaxed, recall an emotion that made you feel uneasy. It can be helpful for you to remember when you felt this and the experience you were having at the time. Take your time and do not rush feeling, allow for your whole self to come on board with this practice.

When and if emotion arises see how long you can remain with the feeling. Observe how it is impacting you. Observe and feel how you are responding in your body, emotions, and thought. As the emotion deepens say the following sentence out loud.

'I am not responsible for making everything better.'

Repeat this as many times as you like until you feel yourself letting go of any expectation.

You are aiming to allow this difficult emotion to be. Feeling it move through you releases it from being a feared aspect of you. If it becomes too uncomfortable take deeper breaths and don't be afraid to cry. When we cry, we bring about transformative energy in the release that crying brings. At any point, you can stop if you feel you have gone as far as you can.

Remain in this space as long as you need. Self-care during this process of opening is essential. Allowing time at the end of this process to be is as important as the process itself. When we feel intense emotion our bodies become heightened and our sensitivity is stronger than normal. This is not something to rush but is part of the process.

You are learning to become comfortable in the discomfort. Breaking through the barrier of inner resistance and restriction will open and free you. This practice heals and empowers you.

Just as you started give yourself time to feel calmer and relaxed before leaving the space. Implement any of the aftercare points in Step Three.

Step Seven:

Incorporating Higher Teachings

All life is moving towards balance and expansion. As inner light grows it also surfaces the deeper blocks that we hold within. When we forget higher potential we remain in the dark. Often we don't know or forget about the true connection that exists between spirit and soul. Instead we divide and separate that which is spiritual over that which is not. We give value to one aspect of ourselves over another. Each time we do this further confusion and discord is created in our being.

The teachings of this book remind us of the higher wisdom of our original state of being. These powerful statements are essential reminders to shake us from the monotony of life.

Take Action:
When you find yourself in-between spaces, either morning or night, when traveling, waiting for

something, before and after meditating, you can take some time to read the teachings section of this book.

To prepare take a few deep breaths. If you wish for a deeper experience repeat awakening the heart in 'Step One'. Start by flicking through the pages of the teachings section and stop where you are drawn. The page that you arrive at will never fail to speak to you.

When you read let go of trying to understand what you read. Repeat each truth slowly. After saying it at least three times allow your whole being to respond. This is a similar process to develop inner knowing in 'Step Four'.

Notice from what you are reading when you feel a response within. You are not looking to connect to everything you read, allow your knowing within to respond. If and when this happens, pause here. An important aspect of this process is not to merely perform the task of reading but to observe how it makes you feel and your experience within after what you have read.

The responses you have matter. Integrating what touches is paramount to your empowerment. Listening to the wisdom of the higher intelligence of your whole being opens you to the truth.

To do this, re-read what touched you and answer the following questions.

What aspect of you is it helping, healing, and empowering?

Why is this important to you?

Take your time to reflect on these questions. Write them down in a diary and explore these meanings for you.

These questions are designed to empower your way of seeing and can be transferred to anything you read and experience in your outer reality. Making life make sense to you is as essential as breathing for the soul and spiritual development.

Step Eight:

Living Truth

In this final step, we summarise the significance of these progressive practices. To live heart centred is a steady and careful path. Many internal and external influences hold us back from living our truth. Pressures, expectations, and the need for external empowerment over inner truth are but a few of the challenges to master.

Each action awakens truth at every level of our being and grows a new stream of life founded upon living light, freedom and the joy in the heart. Who you are matters. To live your truth is to feel your way. The following summary offers perspective and key points in opening you and developing wholeness, empowerment, and completion.

Take Action:

Turning your gaze inwards. 'Steps One' and 'Two' can be done often and will help you alter consciousness quickly. These simple practices build self-awareness.

Our attention has become increasingly fixed on what lies outside of us. Growing connection to our inner world needs us to exercise conscious attention.

Living truth and the healing process are one. Dismissing parts of ourselves has fragmented our soul and created further pain, and resistance to flourish. Turning the tide of indifference and disempowerment starts by relearning about our fragility and sensitivity. We aim to treat vulnerability as we treat our strengths, with value.

Make your experience yours. The light that you carry is released through your truth. Without truth the soul is like a crop starved of water it becomes diminished, drawn, and weak. Reclaiming the true self happens when we create an inner culture based on acceptance, sensitivity, and truth. To fan the fire within begins with what touches you. Live life your way by listening to what touches your heart and follow it. Without meaning, there can be no greater purpose.

Grow trust in your heart to lead you. Losing trust of our inner world has left us feeling empty and barren inside. The prayer in the heart is a great transformational tool. If what we do in life is based upon the sentiments of the heart then we rebuild and recover trust. Growing the connection to the heart force is like rearing a small child. We are learning to develop the unique personality that already resides within us. The heart needs us to listen to it and nurture its unique expression.

Break the habit of keeping things hidden from yourself. When we create an internal culture built on division we inevitably feel uneasy within. One cannot exist free when we encourage parts of ourselves to become more valuable than others. When we create a value system that tries to show a better version of ourselves to the world, we lose the integrity of being. Living truth and allowing the healing process to uncover these hidden parts frees us from this illusion.

Choose to follow what frees your heart. That which is light is the highest expression of care in the world. The joy and tenderness in life known to us as love is truth. This is the embodiment of the heart. When we hear the truth it is like a universal key that we all know. There is an instant acceptance that connects as one. The vibration of truth is felt and accepted by all who also have their heart open. Not everyone is ready as you are to follow light, sometimes to live free we must go ahead alone.

The inner way is vast and unique for all of us. What we understand as spiritual comes in countless and extraordinary ways. We are learning to encourage this freedom of expression in the life we have to live.

Growing one's inner light shines through the truth. Your truth belongs to you only. Without inner light intact, we become overshadowed. The fire in the heart must be strong to overcome the weight of suffering. Sensitivity and the vulnerability of being must not just be allowed but fully accepted as the doorway to the unified self. To open to a greater purpose and expand into the higher potential occurs naturally when the heart is fully open.

As multi-dimensional sentient beings to have health, we must seek to govern all parts of ourselves. We came to create out of ourselves and live this truth into our world. To be free begins from following what touches your heart. Loving what you are and do is not a romantic ideal but answers the burning questions of soul crises. To be spiritual is to know and live love as the cornerstone of our self. Returning to the joy of life is not something we gain outside of us. Joy is in the essence of our being.

Glossary

Every word, when it is pronounced, has its own sound, which derives from within the heart of the speaker. Every word resonates differently depending on who receives it. The glossary seeks to define the essence of each word as it is used in the book according to the author's knowledge in the field of personal empowerment

ACCEPTANCE

When we cling on to, become overly proud and avoid accessing our feelings, acceptance becomes the threshold for release. When we experience total acceptance, we acknowledge what we feel without censorship to the fragility of our true being. Through acceptance, we come to the heart of matter.

BECOMING

Just like a new born baby, we are forever changing, moving and growing. This movement does not stop throughout our existence, since we are in a constant state of becoming and our unique expression is eternally unfolding.

BELIEF

The foundation of the soul is formed from beliefs. It governs actions, thoughts and desires and is the guiding principle of life. Belief from inner-knowing derives from what is intrinsic to one's heart.

CALLING

Often, your calling rises from outside your conscious awareness in the form of a longing that feels like a gravitational pull. It insists that you follow it. It calls for you to bring it to consciousness, to manifest it and to align yourself to its higher teaching.

COMPLETION

Through inner liberation one becomes whole, this is completion. When the inner fire is intact one becomes the master of their reality. One delivers their self from their self, sovereign, free, and empowered.

COURAGE

To have courage is to experience having the openness of a child. Instead of resistance, we accept all that life is offering without expectation. Instead of fear, there is care, instead of conflict; there is hope, which is the essence of courage.

CREATIVE LIFE FORCE

The movement of energy that flows within and without. It is what connects all matter, the communion of life and the embodiment of the eternal fire.

DARK

That which lies in our subconscious state. It is formed from what we do not want to see and is fuelled by fear and rejection. It is the shadow of light. It came into being because of our separation from the oneness state. It transforms through exposure to light, by being seen, which results in the return to wholeness.

DISCORD

A confused state derived from corruption and leads to disharmony of one's inner world. The sense that one is caught, trapped or stuck within their physical, mental, emotional or spiritual reality. Discord remains until inner healing, counsel and release occur.

EMPOWERMENT

The limitations of living the fullness of the self are lifted. Here lies no censorship or restriction to the knowing and expression of one's truth. Where one's belief is authority.

INNER FIRE

When one is free from discord, the creative force of the heart, strength of will, and spirit aligns, realizing the higher potential. When one's fire is intact, the higher good is delivered.

FORGIVENESS

In the act of forgiveness one releases their bind from the limitations of the ego and surrenders to the compassionate expression of love. In this act lies the total acceptance of the fragility of human nature without judgement or conditions.

GOVERNANCE

Mastering the movement of the self from the internal culture of disempowerment to empowerment and completion. This is achieved through the understanding of how the dimensions of the self create reality with the belief that one deliver's the self out of the self.

GRIEF

Grief exists as a process created from the moment we became separated from the oneness state. It is the longing and sorrow in the heart to return to one's true state of being. Its expression remains until inner liberation and completion.

GUILT

Guilt distances us from feeling pain and causes us to disable our authentic responses. It derives from a collective, punitive force that seeks to undermine and threaten one's sovereignty. Guilt offers nothing towards the healing process.

HEART

The sensory organ of the body that calibrates one's being to its higher state. The heart carries the sentient blueprint of the soul by having the capacity to retrieve and integrate the emotional memory of the soul experience from one lifetime to another.

HIGHER-SELF

The higher self embodies the light of one's true expression. It is the most liberated aspect of the soul and is the bridge to the wisdom of the true Spirit.

HOLY

In oneness, the true spirit becomes known through the Holy aspect. It is the governing principle from which God's expression realizes itself consciously through the being of man.

INNER-KNOWING

Inner knowing is the ability to interpret one's truth, which derives from the sensitivity of the heart. One interprets there knowing through the heart to bring it into consciousness.

INTEGRITY

With acceptance of the true nature of their self, one takes full responsibility of their expression. In the knowledge that one is creating their reality in an honest and conscious way, aligned to their truth.

LIGHT

Inner knowing is one's guiding light. Light derives from the highest form of care and is what ignites the fire of one's truth. From the glow of one's truth, it is created.

LOVE

Love unfolds when the heart is free from discord or restriction. Without borders, it is the binding force of all creation, a Holy communion that moves into life without any intention for itself.

ONENESS

Oneness is attained through the fire of completion. This most valued prize of completion is one's natural, pure and perfect state of being. The reality of separation, time, and space exists no more.

PAIN

In the presence of discord, pain is one's natural indicator and warning light that prepares your physical, emotional, mental, and spiritual body for the challenge that lies ahead. It is the gatekeeper that encourages you to pause and to choose consciously to open the door to the unknown. When one surrenders to pain's call, then relief comes.

POTENTIAL

The greater understanding of one's true spirit self. The capacity to hold within one's being the source of God's expression, and to allow it to alter one's consciousness for the highest good.

PRAYER

This is the healing aspect of one's light. It is the concentration of belief that lies in the fire of the heart and that which liberates the hope of man.

PURPOSE

The drive to grow one's self from what touches our hearts and gives us meaning. It is the calling to realize the heart self-aligned with the highest good.

It becomes fully active when maturity of one's light is reached.

REAL

That which is authentic to one's true expression and is without masks, expectation or judgment. You are laid bare and you live what you wish, no matter where it takes you. To live in a real way brings about the greatest opportunity for growth.

SENTIENT

Through the feeling realm one is interconnected to their whole self. One feels their world without restriction and has the ability to integrate through their feeling body, all that they experience.

SHADOW

The shadow lies within one's subconscious fears. It acts upon the conscious self in order to become transmuted to light. It activates the inner movement towards healing the fragmented self towards wholeness. It is an essential component for healing.

SHAME

When corruption lies within, shame becomes empowered. Its purpose is to awaken our deeper consciousness and encourage us to bow in humility at our own feet and reunite with the core of our true self.

It is the call to accept pain and to move through the suffering of our fall.

SHINING

The joy of living unlimited from the opening of one's true expression. When one experiences the truest state of being, the essence of one's self shines the brightest.

SHOWING

When the presence of oneself is intact and centred, then the expression of one's light can be shown to the world. In the face of fear or judgment one is able to express their truth with honesty and integrity.

SOVEREIGNTY

One's sovereignty comes through the realisation of their true being. In every aspect of the self, one is free, the authority and master of their reality.

SURRENDER

When there lays no resistance to the struggle of one's fall, there is the surrender to life processes. Instead of the wish to control one's experience, to surrender produces the state of grace and torment ceases to be.

TRUE SELF

When one is free to experience the fullness of their self, unrestricted, then the fire within the heart is ignited.

The expression of what one truly is becomes free to be realised.

TRUST

It is the reassurance that the heart is being held, regardless of the absence of oneness. It is the unbreakable pact between man and creation, the knowing that one's path is the journey to eternal light. Through life's struggle, one comes to know they are not a victim or being punished but through it, life is willing you to be free.

TRUTH

What is real within is truth. Truth bridges the soul to the essence of the eternal Spirit. Through living truth, one is untied from the illusions of life. Truth is the master liberator.

VULNERABILITY

Through facing one's pain, there is the experience of the fragility of one's sensitivity. This fragility lasts as long as is needed to recover one's truth and to find the way forward. This state is a necessary holding space to allow for the transition of reopening one's heart, integrating new knowledge of oneself and awakening to a higher potential.

WHOLENESS

One's perfect state where there is no seeking, since all aspects of oneself are intact, true and clear. No parts of oneself are fragmented or tethered. In this state lies the ultimate knowing that one's path is founded not on survival but as a complete, whole, and self-sufficient being.

WISDOM

Wisdom is the counterpart of truth and is its conscious expression. Truth carries wisdom as its source and brings it into the world in an accessible way.

WISH

Where there is a longing in the heart, for it to manifest one first elevates it to the place of dreaming and imagination, where all is possible. It is then that this seed is sown in the heart to be given higher blessing towards its fruition. From here the longing in the heart becomes the wish.

About the Author

Kefah Bates has over twenty years of experience working within the field of healing and empowerment. She teaches self-governance, the core truths of soul crises, and the nature of the unlimited self.

Born to Yemeni parents, she grew up in the county of Staffordshire, England. She studied creative arts at university and from there went on to complete teacher training for higher education. Her passion for supporting other's well-being began when working within communities based on the philosophical teachings of Rudolph Steiner. For over seven years, she immersed herself in esoteric knowledge and practice.

Her life took a new course when she moved from England to Edinburgh. Wanting to further her understanding of the whole self, she trained in TA Counselling and completed Ashtanga Yoga Teacher Certification. Her love of learning about personal development and spiritual growth continued with a passion as she went on to qualify in the healing modalities of Reiki, Energy, and Shamanic Healing. After years of study and practice she had developed strong foundations to grow her calling to understand why suffering exists in herself and others.

With relentless dedication, she ran a healing centre supporting people through their pain and trauma. Over the next twelve years, she would deliver regular workshops and courses on spiritual development, healing, and qualifying others to become healers. She became devoted to celebrating the spirit of nature and wildlife with crafts by facilitating ceremonies to honour the passing of seasons.

Profound inner transformations led her to make a life-long commitment as a spiritual teacher. Kefah now travels worldwide teaching, speaking, and writing on the importance of governing the self, healing, and empowerment. She presently resides and works in Bali.

.~.

www.kefahbates.com